GRATITUDE
JOURNAL

FINDING HAPPINESS AND JOY
IN 5 MINUTES A DAY

A 52-week guide to cultivating
an attitude of gratitude

Your Name

Gratitude Journal: Finding Happiness and Joy in 5 Minutes a Day
Copyright 2017 by Devin C. Hughes

ISBN-13: 978-1986742207
ISBN-10: 1986742202

Produced for use by
Devin C. Hughes Enterprises, LLC
March 2018

Book design:
Elizabeth Beeton
B10 Mediaworx

If you think happiness matters and want to be part of creating a happier society for everyone, then join thousands of others at www.devinchughes.com.

INTRODUCTION

The benefits of practicing gratitude are nearly endless. People who regularly practice gratitude by taking time to notice and reflect upon the things they're thankful for experience more positive emotions, feel more alive, sleep better, express more compassion and kindness, and even have stronger immune systems.

The best way to reap the benefits of gratitude is to notice new things you're grateful for every day. Gratitude journaling works because it slowly changes the way we perceive situations by adjusting what we focus on.

AT TIMES OUR OWN LIGHT GOES
OUT AND IS REKINDLED BY A SPARK
FROM ANOTHER PERSON.
EACH OF US HAS CAUSE TO THINK
WITH DEEP GRATITUDE OF THOSE
WHO HAVE LIGHTED THE FLAME
WITHIN US.
— ALBERT SCHWEITZER

ABOUT THIS JOURNAL

There's no wrong way to keep a gratitude journal, but here are some general instructions to you get started.

Write down up to 3-5 things for which you feel grateful. The physical record is important—don't just do this exercise in your head. The things you list can be relatively small in importance ("The high-five I got from my boss today during the staff meeting.") or relatively large ("My daughter got accepted into the college of her dreams."). The goal of the exercise is to remember a good event, experience, person, or thing in your life—then enjoy the good emotions that come with it.

As you write, here are nine important tips:

1. Be as specific as possible—specificity is key to fostering gratitude.

2. Go for depth over breadth. Elaborating in detail about a particular person or thing for which you're grateful carries more benefits than a superficial list of many things.

3. Get personal. Focusing on people to whom you are grateful has more of an impact than focusing on things for which you are grateful.

4. Try subtraction, not just addition. Consider what your life would be like without certain people or things, rather than just tallying up all the good stuff.

5. See good things as "gifts." Thinking of the good things in your life as gifts guards against taking them for granted. Try to relish and savor the gifts you've received.

6. Savor surprises. Try to record events that were unexpected or surprising, as these tend to elicit stronger levels of gratitude.

7. Write regularly. Whether you write every other day or once a week, commit to a regular time to journal, then honor that commitment.

GRATITUDE BLOCKS
TOXIC EMOTIONS,
SUCH AS ENVY,
RESENTMENT, REGRET
AND DEPRESSION,
WHICH CAN DESTROY
OUR HAPPINESS.

ROBERT EMMONS

MONTH 1
PONDER

3 to 5 things for which you are currently grateful, from the mundane (your dryer is fixed, your flowers are finally in bloom, your husband remembered to stop by the store) to the magnificent (your child's first steps, the beauty of the sky at night).

WEEKLY GRATITUDE JOURNAL

Ponder 3 – 5 things for which you are currently grateful.

Sunday _____

_____

Monday _____

_____

Tuesday _____

_____

Wednesday _____

_____

Thursday _____

_____

Friday _____

_____

Saturday _____

_____

WEEKLY GRATITUDE JOURNAL

Ponder 3 – 5 things for which you are currently grateful.

Sunday _____

_____
_____
_____
_____
_____
_____

Monday _____

_____
_____
_____
_____
_____

Tuesday _____

_____
_____
_____
_____
_____

Wednesday _____

_____
_____
_____
_____
_____

Thursday _____

_____
_____
_____
_____
_____

Friday _____

_____
_____
_____
_____
_____

Saturday _____

_____
_____
_____
_____
_____

WEEKLY GRATITUDE JOURNAL

Ponder 3 – 5 things for which you are currently grateful.

Sunday _____

_____
_____
_____
_____
_____

Monday _____

_____
_____
_____
_____
_____

Tuesday _____

_____
_____
_____
_____
_____

Wednesday _____

_____
_____
_____
_____
_____

Thursday _____

_____
_____
_____
_____
_____

Friday _____

_____
_____
_____
_____
_____

Saturday _____

_____
_____
_____
_____
_____

WEEKLY GRATITUDE JOURNAL

Ponder 3 – 5 things for which you are currently grateful.

Sunday _____

_____
_____
_____
_____
_____
_____

Monday _____

_____
_____
_____
_____
_____
_____

Tuesday _____

_____
_____
_____
_____
_____
_____

Wednesday _____

_____
_____
_____
_____
_____
_____

Thursday _____

_____
_____
_____
_____
_____

Friday _____

_____
_____
_____
_____
_____

Saturday _____

_____
_____
_____
_____
_____
_____

KIND HEARTS ARE THE GARDENS.

KIND THOUGHTS ARE THE ROOTS.

KIND WORDS ARE THE BLOSSOMS.

KIND DEEDS ARE THE FRUITS.

KIRPAL SINGH

MONTH 2
PONDER

3 to 5 acts of kindness you can show, did show, or have been shown.

How did those acts make you feel and impact your life?

WEEKLY GRATITUDE JOURNAL

Ponder 3 – 5 acts of kindness you can show, did show, or have been shown.
How did those acts make you feel and impact your life?

Sunday _____

_____
_____
_____
_____
_____
_____

Monday _____

_____
_____
_____
_____
_____
_____

Tuesday _____

_____
_____
_____
_____
_____
_____

Wednesday _____

_____
_____
_____
_____
_____
_____

Thursday _____

_____
_____
_____
_____
_____
_____

Friday _____

_____
_____
_____
_____
_____
_____

Saturday _____

_____
_____
_____
_____
_____
_____

WEEKLY GRATITUDE JOURNAL

Ponder 3 – 5 acts of kindness you can show, did show, or have been shown.
How did those acts make you feel and impact your life?

Sunday _____

_____
_____
_____
_____
_____

Monday _____

_____
_____
_____
_____
_____

Tuesday _____

_____
_____
_____
_____
_____

Wednesday _____

_____
_____
_____
_____
_____

Thursday _____

_____
_____
_____
_____
_____

Friday _____

_____
_____
_____
_____
_____

Saturday _____

_____
_____
_____
_____
_____

WEEKLY GRATITUDE JOURNAL

Ponder 3 – 5 acts of kindness you can show, did show, or have been shown.
How did those acts make you feel and impact your life?

Sunday _____

_____
_____
_____
_____
_____
_____

Monday _____

_____
_____
_____
_____
_____
_____

Tuesday _____

_____
_____
_____
_____
_____
_____

Wednesday _____

_____
_____
_____
_____
_____
_____

Thursday _____

_____
_____
_____
_____
_____
_____

Friday _____

_____
_____
_____
_____
_____
_____

Saturday _____

_____
_____
_____
_____
_____
_____

WEEKLY GRATITUDE JOURNAL

Ponder 3 – 5 acts of kindness you can show, did show, or have been shown.
How did those acts make you feel and impact your life?

Sunday _____

_____
_____
_____
_____
_____

Monday _____

_____
_____
_____
_____
_____

Tuesday _____

_____
_____
_____
_____
_____

Wednesday _____

_____
_____
_____
_____
_____

Thursday _____

_____
_____
_____
_____
_____

Friday _____

_____
_____
_____
_____
_____

Saturday _____

_____
_____
_____
_____
_____

FEELING GRATITUDE
AND NOT EXPRESSING
IT IS LIKE WRAPPING A
PRESENT AND NOT
GIVING IT.

WILLIAM ARTHUR WARD

MONTH 3
WRITE.

Write a note or send an email or text to someone at work or friend or family [every day this month] and tell them how grateful you are for them being in your life.

WEEKLY GRATITUDE JOURNAL

Write a note to someone every day this month
to express your gratitude for their presence in your life.

Sunday _____

Monday _____

Tuesday _____

Wednesday _____

Thursday _____

Friday _____

Saturday _____

WEEKLY GRATITUDE JOURNAL

Write a note to someone every day this month
to express your gratitude for their presence in your life.

Sunday _____

_____
_____
_____
_____
_____
_____

Monday _____

_____
_____
_____
_____
_____
_____

Tuesday _____

_____
_____
_____
_____
_____
_____

Wednesday _____

_____
_____
_____
_____
_____
_____

Thursday _____

_____
_____
_____
_____
_____
_____

Friday _____

_____
_____
_____
_____
_____
_____

Saturday _____

_____
_____
_____
_____
_____
_____

WEEKLY GRATITUDE JOURNAL

Write a note to someone every day this month
to express your gratitude for their presence in your life.

Sunday _____

_____
_____
_____
_____
_____
_____

Monday _____

_____
_____
_____
_____
_____
_____

Tuesday _____

_____
_____
_____
_____
_____
_____

Wednesday _____

_____
_____
_____
_____
_____
_____

Thursday _____

_____
_____
_____
_____
_____
_____

Friday _____

_____
_____
_____
_____
_____
_____

Saturday _____

_____
_____
_____
_____
_____
_____

WEEKLY GRATITUDE JOURNAL

Write a note to someone every day this month
to express your gratitude for their presence in your life.

Sunday _____

_____
_____
_____
_____
_____
_____

Monday _____

_____
_____
_____
_____
_____
_____

Tuesday _____

_____
_____
_____
_____
_____
_____

Wednesday _____

_____
_____
_____
_____
_____
_____

Thursday _____

_____
_____
_____
_____
_____
_____

Friday _____

_____
_____
_____
_____
_____
_____

Saturday _____

_____
_____
_____
_____
_____
_____

WE OFTEN TAKE FOR
GRANTED THE VERY
THINGS THAT MOST
DESERVE OUR
GRATITUDE.

CYNTHIA OZICK

MONTH 4
SEE.

This month,
find pictures and
sayings that remind
you to be grateful and
hang a few.

WEEKLY GRATITUDE JOURNAL

Hang pictures that remind you to be grateful.

Sunday _____

_____
_____
_____
_____
_____
_____

Monday _____

_____
_____
_____
_____
_____
_____

Tuesday _____

_____
_____
_____
_____
_____
_____

Wednesday _____

_____
_____
_____
_____
_____
_____

Thursday _____

_____
_____
_____
_____
_____
_____

Friday _____

_____
_____
_____
_____
_____
_____

Saturday _____

_____
_____
_____
_____
_____
_____

WEEKLY GRATITUDE JOURNAL

Hang pictures that remind you to be grateful.

Sunday _____

_____
_____
_____
_____
_____
_____

Monday _____

_____
_____
_____
_____
_____
_____

Tuesday _____

_____
_____
_____
_____
_____
_____

Wednesday _____

_____
_____
_____
_____
_____
_____

Thursday _____

_____
_____
_____
_____
_____
_____

Friday _____

_____
_____
_____
_____
_____
_____

Saturday _____

_____
_____
_____
_____
_____
_____

WEEKLY GRATITUDE JOURNAL

Hang pictures that remind you to be grateful.

Sunday _____

_____
_____
_____
_____
_____

Monday _____

_____
_____
_____
_____
_____

Tuesday _____

_____
_____
_____
_____
_____

Wednesday _____

_____
_____
_____
_____
_____

Thursday _____

_____
_____
_____
_____
_____

Friday _____

_____
_____
_____
_____
_____

Saturday _____

_____
_____
_____
_____
_____

WEEKLY GRATITUDE JOURNAL

Hang pictures that remind you to be grateful.

Sunday _____

_____
_____
_____
_____
_____
_____

Monday _____

_____
_____
_____
_____
_____
_____

Tuesday _____

_____
_____
_____
_____
_____
_____

Wednesday _____

_____
_____
_____
_____
_____
_____

Thursday _____

_____
_____
_____
_____
_____
_____

Friday _____

_____
_____
_____
_____
_____
_____

Saturday _____

_____
_____
_____
_____
_____
_____

SO MUCH HAS BEEN
GIVEN TO ME, I HAVE
NO TIME TO PONDER
OVER THAT WHICH
HAS BEEN DENIED.

HELEN KELLER

MONTH 5
BUILD A
GRATITUDE JAR.

Each day, write down one thing you are grateful for [bonus for colored paper!] and put it in a jar.

At the end of the month, open the jar and read the notes to feel grateful all over again.

WEEKLY GRATITUDE JOURNAL

Each day, write down one thing you are grateful for and put it in a jar.

Sunday _____

_____
_____
_____
_____
_____
_____

Monday _____

_____
_____
_____
_____
_____
_____

Tuesday _____

_____
_____
_____
_____
_____
_____

Wednesday _____

_____
_____
_____
_____
_____
_____

Thursday _____

_____
_____
_____
_____
_____
_____

Friday _____

_____
_____
_____
_____
_____
_____

Saturday _____

_____
_____
_____
_____
_____
_____

WEEKLY GRATITUDE JOURNAL

Each day, write down one thing you are grateful for and put it in a jar.

Sunday _____

_____
_____
_____
_____
_____
_____

Monday _____

_____
_____
_____
_____
_____
_____

Tuesday _____

_____
_____
_____
_____
_____
_____

Wednesday _____

_____
_____
_____
_____
_____
_____

Thursday _____

_____
_____
_____
_____
_____
_____

Friday _____

_____
_____
_____
_____
_____
_____

Saturday _____

_____
_____
_____
_____
_____
_____

WEEKLY GRATITUDE JOURNAL

Each day, write down one thing you are grateful for and put it in a jar.

Sunday _____

_____
_____
_____
_____
_____
_____

Monday _____

_____
_____
_____
_____
_____
_____

Tuesday _____

_____
_____
_____
_____
_____
_____

Wednesday _____

_____
_____
_____
_____
_____
_____

Thursday _____

_____
_____
_____
_____
_____
_____

Friday _____

_____
_____
_____
_____
_____
_____

Saturday _____

_____
_____
_____
_____
_____
_____

WEEKLY GRATITUDE JOURNAL

Each day, write down one thing you are grateful for and put it in a jar.

Sunday _____

_____
_____
_____
_____
_____
_____

Monday _____

_____
_____
_____
_____
_____
_____

Tuesday _____

_____
_____
_____
_____
_____
_____

Wednesday _____

_____
_____
_____
_____
_____
_____

Thursday _____

_____
_____
_____
_____
_____
_____

Friday _____

_____
_____
_____
_____
_____
_____

Saturday _____

_____
_____
_____
_____
_____
_____

IF THE ONLY PRAYER
YOU SAID IN YOUR
WHOLE LIFE WAS
"THANK YOU," THAT
WOULD SUFFICE.

MEISTER ECKHART

MONTH 6
PRACTICE A
GRATITUDE RITUAL.

Some people say grace before a meal. Pausing in gratitude before eating doesn't have to be religious. It's a simple habit that helps us notice and appreciate the blessing of food on the table.

WEEKLY GRATITUDE JOURNAL

Practice a Gratitude Ritual. Pause in gratitude before acting
to notice and appreciate the blessing in front of you.

Sunday _____

_____
_____
_____
_____
_____
_____

Monday _____

_____
_____
_____
_____
_____
_____

Tuesday _____

_____
_____
_____
_____
_____
_____

Wednesday _____

_____
_____
_____
_____
_____
_____

Thursday _____

_____
_____
_____
_____
_____
_____

Friday _____

_____
_____
_____
_____
_____
_____

Saturday _____

_____
_____
_____
_____
_____

WEEKLY GRATITUDE JOURNAL

Practice a Gratitude Ritual. Pause in gratitude before acting
to notice and appreciate the blessing in front of you.

Sunday _____

_____
_____
_____
_____
_____
_____

Monday _____

_____
_____
_____
_____
_____
_____

Tuesday _____

_____
_____
_____
_____
_____
_____

Wednesday _____

_____
_____
_____
_____
_____
_____

Thursday _____

_____
_____
_____
_____
_____
_____

Friday _____

_____
_____
_____
_____
_____
_____

Saturday _____

_____
_____
_____
_____
_____
_____

WEEKLY GRATITUDE JOURNAL

Practice a Gratitude Ritual. Pause in gratitude before acting
to notice and appreciate the blessing in front of you.

Sunday _____

_____
_____
_____
_____
_____
_____

Monday _____

_____
_____
_____
_____
_____
_____

Tuesday _____

_____
_____
_____
_____
_____
_____

Wednesday _____

_____
_____
_____
_____
_____
_____

Thursday _____

_____
_____
_____
_____
_____
_____

Friday _____

_____
_____
_____
_____
_____
_____

Saturday _____

_____
_____
_____
_____
_____
_____

WEEKLY GRATITUDE JOURNAL

Practice a Gratitude Ritual. Pause in gratitude before acting
to notice and appreciate the blessing in front of you.

Sunday _____

_____
_____
_____
_____
_____

Monday _____

_____
_____
_____
_____
_____

Tuesday _____

_____
_____
_____
_____
_____

Wednesday _____

_____
_____
_____
_____
_____

Thursday _____

_____
_____
_____
_____
_____

Friday _____

_____
_____
_____
_____
_____

Saturday _____

_____
_____
_____
_____
_____

NO ONE WHO
ACHIEVES SUCCESS
DOES SO WITHOUT
ACKNOWLEDGING THE
HELP OF OTHERS.

THE WISE AND
CONFIDENT
ACKNOWLEDGE THIS
HELP WITH GRATITUDE.

ALFRED NORTH WHITEHEAD

MONTH 7
SHOW

your appreciation to someone who did something nice at work

"It was really kind of you to...," "It really helped me out when you...," "You did me a big favor when...," will go a long way toward your own happiness.

WEEKLY GRATITUDE JOURNAL

Show your appreciation to someone who did something nice at work.

Sunday _____

_____
_____
_____
_____
_____
_____

Monday _____

_____
_____
_____
_____
_____
_____

Tuesday _____

_____
_____
_____
_____
_____
_____

Wednesday _____

_____
_____
_____
_____
_____
_____

Thursday _____

_____
_____
_____
_____
_____
_____

Friday _____

_____
_____
_____
_____
_____
_____

Saturday _____

_____
_____
_____
_____
_____
_____

WEEKLY GRATITUDE JOURNAL

Show your appreciation to someone who did something nice at work.

Sunday _____

_____
_____
_____
_____
_____
_____

Monday _____

_____
_____
_____
_____
_____
_____

Tuesday _____

_____
_____
_____
_____
_____
_____

Wednesday _____

_____
_____
_____
_____
_____
_____

Thursday _____

_____
_____
_____
_____
_____
_____

Friday _____

_____
_____
_____
_____
_____
_____

Saturday _____

_____
_____
_____
_____
_____
_____

WEEKLY GRATITUDE JOURNAL

Show your appreciation to someone who did something nice at work.

Sunday _____

_____
_____
_____
_____
_____
_____

Monday _____

_____
_____
_____
_____
_____
_____

Tuesday _____

_____
_____
_____
_____
_____
_____

Wednesday _____

_____
_____
_____
_____
_____
_____

Thursday _____

_____
_____
_____
_____
_____
_____

Friday _____

_____
_____
_____
_____
_____
_____

Saturday _____

_____
_____
_____
_____
_____
_____

WEEKLY GRATITUDE JOURNAL

Show your appreciation to someone who did something nice at work.

Sunday _____

_____
_____
_____
_____
_____
_____

Monday _____

_____
_____
_____
_____
_____
_____

Tuesday _____

_____
_____
_____
_____
_____
_____

Wednesday _____

_____
_____
_____
_____
_____
_____

Thursday _____

_____
_____
_____
_____
_____
_____

Friday _____

_____
_____
_____
_____
_____
_____

Saturday _____

_____
_____
_____
_____
_____
_____

ONE OF THE MOST
IMPORTANT THINGS
YOU CAN DO ON THIS
EARTH IS TO LET
PEOPLE KNOW THEY
ARE NOT ALONE.

SHANNON L. ALDER

MONTH 8
CALL

a friend or family
member every day to
touch base, say hello,
and re-connect.

WEEKLY GRATITUDE JOURNAL

Call a friend or family member every day to say hello and re-connect.

Sunday _____

_____
_____
_____
_____
_____

Monday _____

_____
_____
_____
_____
_____

Tuesday _____

_____
_____
_____
_____
_____

Wednesday _____

_____
_____
_____
_____
_____

Thursday _____

_____
_____
_____
_____
_____

Friday _____

_____
_____
_____
_____
_____

Saturday _____

_____
_____
_____
_____
_____

WEEKLY GRATITUDE JOURNAL

Call a friend or family member every day to say hello and re-connect.

Sunday _____

_____
_____
_____
_____
_____

Monday _____

_____
_____
_____
_____
_____

Tuesday _____

_____
_____
_____
_____
_____

Wednesday _____

_____
_____
_____
_____
_____

Thursday _____

_____
_____
_____
_____
_____

Friday _____

_____
_____
_____
_____
_____

Saturday _____

_____
_____
_____
_____
_____

WEEKLY GRATITUDE JOURNAL

Call a friend or family member every day to say hello and re-connect.

Sunday _____

_____
_____
_____
_____
_____

Monday _____

_____
_____
_____
_____
_____

Tuesday _____

_____
_____
_____
_____
_____

Wednesday _____

_____
_____
_____
_____
_____

Thursday _____

_____
_____
_____
_____
_____

Friday _____

_____
_____
_____
_____
_____

Saturday _____

_____
_____
_____
_____
_____

WEEKLY GRATITUDE JOURNAL

Call a friend or family member every day to say hello and re-connect.

Sunday _____

_____
_____
_____
_____
_____
_____

Monday _____

_____
_____
_____
_____
_____
_____

Tuesday _____

_____
_____
_____
_____
_____
_____

Wednesday _____

_____
_____
_____
_____
_____
_____

Thursday _____

_____
_____
_____
_____
_____
_____

Friday _____

_____
_____
_____
_____
_____
_____

Saturday _____

_____
_____
_____
_____
_____
_____

IT'S ALWAYS THE
COMPLIMENTS FROM
PEOPLE YOU LOVE
THAT MEAN SO MUCH.

MARIA BAMFORD

MONTH 9
GRATITUDE BOX

Decorate a small box.
Ponder a friend or
loved one.
Write what you
appreciate about this
person on a pretty
piece of paper and put
it in the box.
Give the box to that
person.

WEEKLY GRATITUDE JOURNAL

Every day, write an appreciative note to a loved one or friend,
collect them in a pretty box, and give it to them at the end of the month.

Sunday _____

Monday _____

Tuesday _____

Wednesday _____

Thursday _____

Friday _____

Saturday _____

WEEKLY GRATITUDE JOURNAL

Every day, write an appreciative note to a loved one or friend,
collect them in a pretty box, and give it to them at the end of the month.

Sunday _____

_____
_____
_____
_____
_____

Monday _____

_____
_____
_____
_____
_____

Tuesday _____

_____
_____
_____
_____
_____

Wednesday _____

_____
_____
_____
_____
_____

Thursday _____

_____
_____
_____
_____
_____

Friday _____

_____
_____
_____
_____
_____

Saturday _____

_____
_____
_____
_____
_____

WEEKLY GRATITUDE JOURNAL

Every day, write an appreciative note to a loved one or friend,
collect them in a pretty box, and give it to them at the end of the month.

Sunday _____

_____
_____
_____
_____
_____
_____

Monday _____

_____
_____
_____
_____
_____
_____

Tuesday _____

_____
_____
_____
_____
_____
_____

Wednesday _____

_____
_____
_____
_____
_____
_____

Thursday _____

_____
_____
_____
_____
_____
_____

Friday _____

_____
_____
_____
_____
_____
_____

Saturday _____

_____
_____
_____
_____
_____
_____

WEEKLY GRATITUDE JOURNAL

Every day, write an appreciative note to a loved one or friend,
collect them in a pretty box, and give it to them at the end of the month.

Sunday _____

_____
_____
_____
_____
_____

Monday _____

_____
_____
_____
_____
_____

Tuesday _____

_____
_____
_____
_____
_____

Wednesday _____

_____
_____
_____
_____
_____

Thursday _____

_____
_____
_____
_____
_____

Friday _____

_____
_____
_____
_____
_____

Saturday _____

_____
_____
_____
_____
_____

THE BEST WAY
TO PAY FOR A
LOVELY MOMENT
IS TO ENJOY IT.

RICHARD BACH

MONTH 10
GRATITUDE WALK.

Take a walk to find the
things you are grateful
for in your life.

WEEKLY GRATITUDE JOURNAL

Take a walk to find the things you are grateful for in your life.

Sunday _____

_____
_____
_____
_____
_____

Monday _____

_____
_____
_____
_____
_____

Tuesday _____

_____
_____
_____
_____
_____

Wednesday _____

_____
_____
_____
_____
_____

Thursday _____

_____
_____
_____
_____
_____

Friday _____

_____
_____
_____
_____
_____

Saturday _____

_____
_____
_____
_____
_____

WEEKLY GRATITUDE JOURNAL

Take a walk to find the things you are grateful for in your life.

Sunday _____

_____
_____
_____
_____
_____

Monday _____

_____
_____
_____
_____
_____

Tuesday _____

_____
_____
_____
_____
_____

Wednesday _____

_____
_____
_____
_____
_____

Thursday _____

_____
_____
_____
_____
_____

Friday _____

_____
_____
_____
_____
_____

Saturday _____

_____
_____
_____
_____
_____

WEEKLY GRATITUDE JOURNAL

Take a walk to find the things you are grateful for in your life.

Sunday _____

_____
_____
_____
_____
_____
_____

Monday _____

_____
_____
_____
_____
_____
_____

Tuesday _____

_____
_____
_____
_____
_____
_____

Wednesday _____

_____
_____
_____
_____
_____
_____

Thursday _____

_____
_____
_____
_____
_____

Friday _____

_____
_____
_____
_____
_____

Saturday _____

_____
_____
_____
_____
_____
_____

WEEKLY GRATITUDE JOURNAL

Take a walk to find the things you are grateful for in your life.

Sunday _____

_____
_____
_____
_____
_____
_____

Monday _____

_____
_____
_____
_____
_____
_____

Tuesday _____

_____
_____
_____
_____
_____
_____

Wednesday _____

_____
_____
_____
_____
_____
_____

Thursday _____

_____
_____
_____
_____
_____
_____

Friday _____

_____
_____
_____
_____
_____
_____

Saturday _____

_____
_____
_____
_____
_____
_____

APPRECIATION IS A
WONDERFUL THING.
IT MAKES WHAT IS
EXCELLENT IN OTHERS
BELONG TO US AS
WELL.

VOLTAIRE

MONTH 11
GRATITUDE VISIT.

Think about a person who has recently done something good for you, to whom you have not yet expressed your gratitude.

Seek them out and tell them in person.

WEEKLY GRATITUDE JOURNAL

Visit someone to express your gratitude for them and why.

Sunday _____

_____
_____
_____
_____
_____
_____

Monday _____

_____
_____
_____
_____
_____
_____

Tuesday _____

_____
_____
_____
_____
_____
_____

Wednesday _____

_____
_____
_____
_____
_____
_____

Thursday _____

_____
_____
_____
_____
_____
_____

Friday _____

_____
_____
_____
_____
_____
_____

Saturday _____

_____
_____
_____
_____
_____
_____

WEEKLY GRATITUDE JOURNAL

Visit someone to express your gratitude for them and why.

Sunday _____

_____
_____
_____
_____
_____

Monday _____

_____
_____
_____
_____
_____

Tuesday _____

_____
_____
_____
_____
_____

Wednesday _____

_____
_____
_____
_____
_____

Thursday _____

_____
_____
_____
_____
_____

Friday _____

_____
_____
_____
_____
_____

Saturday _____

_____
_____
_____
_____
_____

WEEKLY GRATITUDE JOURNAL

Visit someone to express your gratitude for them and why.

Sunday _____

_____
_____
_____
_____
_____
_____

Monday _____

_____
_____
_____
_____
_____
_____

Tuesday _____

_____
_____
_____
_____
_____
_____

Wednesday _____

_____
_____
_____
_____
_____
_____

Thursday _____

_____
_____
_____
_____
_____
_____

Friday _____

_____
_____
_____
_____
_____
_____

Saturday _____

_____
_____
_____
_____
_____
_____

WEEKLY GRATITUDE JOURNAL

Visit someone to express your gratitude for them and why.

Sunday _____

_____
_____
_____
_____
_____
_____

Monday _____

_____
_____
_____
_____
_____
_____

Tuesday _____

_____
_____
_____
_____
_____
_____

Wednesday _____

_____
_____
_____
_____
_____
_____

Thursday _____

_____
_____
_____
_____
_____
_____

Friday _____

_____
_____
_____
_____
_____
_____

Saturday _____

_____
_____
_____
_____
_____
_____

WHEN WE GIVE
CHEERFULLY AND
ACCEPT GRATEFULLY,
EVERYONE IS BLESSED.

MAYA ANGELOU

MONTH 12
GRATITUDE DINNER.

Every day, think of
your closest friends
and why you
appreciate them.

Host a dinner party in
honor of your closest
friends to show your
appreciation for each
other.

WEEKLY GRATITUDE JOURNAL

Every day, think of your closest friends and why you appreciate them,
then plan a dinner party in their honor.

Sunday _____

_____
_____
_____
_____
_____
_____

Monday _____

_____
_____
_____
_____
_____
_____

Tuesday _____

_____
_____
_____
_____
_____
_____

Wednesday _____

_____
_____
_____
_____
_____
_____

Thursday _____

_____
_____
_____
_____
_____
_____

Friday _____

_____
_____
_____
_____
_____
_____

Saturday _____

_____
_____
_____
_____
_____
_____

WEEKLY GRATITUDE JOURNAL

Every day, think of your closest friends and why you appreciate them,
then plan a dinner party in their honor.

Sunday _____

_____
_____
_____
_____
_____
_____

Monday _____

_____
_____
_____
_____
_____
_____

Tuesday _____

_____
_____
_____
_____
_____
_____

Wednesday _____

_____
_____
_____
_____
_____
_____

Thursday _____

_____
_____
_____
_____
_____
_____

Friday _____

_____
_____
_____
_____
_____
_____

Saturday _____

_____
_____
_____
_____
_____
_____

WEEKLY GRATITUDE JOURNAL

Every day, think of your closest friends and why you appreciate them,
then plan a dinner party in their honor.

Sunday _____

_____
_____
_____
_____
_____
_____

Monday _____

_____
_____
_____
_____
_____
_____

Tuesday _____

_____
_____
_____
_____
_____
_____

Wednesday _____

_____
_____
_____
_____
_____
_____

Thursday _____

_____
_____
_____
_____
_____

Friday _____

_____
_____
_____
_____
_____

Saturday _____

_____
_____
_____
_____
_____

WEEKLY GRATITUDE JOURNAL

Every day, think of your closest friends and why you appreciate them,
then plan a dinner party in their honor.

Sunday _____

_____
_____
_____
_____
_____
_____

Monday _____

_____
_____
_____
_____
_____
_____

Tuesday _____

_____
_____
_____
_____
_____
_____

Wednesday _____

_____
_____
_____
_____
_____
_____

Thursday _____

_____
_____
_____
_____
_____
_____

Friday _____

_____
_____
_____
_____
_____
_____

Saturday _____

_____
_____
_____
_____
_____
_____

THE SCIENCE OF GRATITUDE

It may seem funny to think that there is actual science behind gratitude. How can something like that be studied? How can it be quantified? Despite these understandably abstract ideas, there is a great deal of scientific proof that gratitude is a beneficial practice that can have a major impact on people's happiness and perception of life in general.

What is Gratitude?

As so simply and eloquently defined by Merriam-Webster, gratitude is a feeling of appreciation or thanks. Pretty straightforward, right? It may seem that way at first glance, but when you delve further into it, gratitude is a complex series of emotions that can even trigger physical sensations. It's a whole-being reaction.

The Emotional and Mental Effects of Gratitude

It's obvious that when you show gratitude to another the recipient usually feels good about the interaction – but did you know that it has a whole bunch of great benefits for you, too? Even if you're not grateful towards someone, but just grateful for something (for example, your home), you are sending feel-good signals to your brain. Here are just some of the ways that gratitude can improve your emotional and mental health.

> • **Increases Happiness.** Showing gratitude can make you happier – gratitude researcher Robert Emmons found that, "Gratitude blocks toxic emotions, such as envy, resentment, regret, and depression, which can destroy our happiness." Considering these are some of the biggest emotional complaints of many people, it wouldn't hurt to incorporate gratitude into daily routines.

> • **Improves Clinical Depression.** When asked to write a letter of gratitude, suicidal inpatients

experienced a decrease in their feelings of hopelessness by 88 percent, and 94 percent experienced an increase in their level of optimism.

• **Delivers More Focus and Energy.** Students who were taught self-guided gratitude exercises reported a higher level of energy, enthusiasm, alertness, determination, and attentiveness compared to those who focused on difficulties and failed to acknowledge the positive aspects of their lives.

Gratitude has so many far-reaching benefits for emotional and mental health that entire books have been written on the topic. It is no wonder pastors, mental health specialists, teachers, and crisis prevention workers are implementing this incredible tool.

The Physical Effects of Gratitude

After countless hours of scientific study and observation, it has become clear that showing gratitude can improve your physical as well as your mental well-being.

• **Better Sleep.** According to the CDC, Americans are an overly-tired nation, with close to 30 percent of Americans getting less than adequate amounts of sleep. However, it's been found that people who mindfully practice gratitude regularly get more and better quality sleep.

Additionally, an article from UC-Davis Health System notes that "Gratitude is related to a 10-percent improvement in sleep quality in patients with chronic pain, 76 percent of whom had insomnia, and 19 percent lower depression levels." This is pretty significant considering the number of people who suffer from sleep-related disorders.

• **Lower Cortisol Levels.** The stress hormone cortisol can wreak havoc on even the healthiest individuals, making them feel tired and dampening their immune systems. This opens individuals up to a greater number of pathogens they would normally be able to fight off. However, it has been found that cortisol levels are 23% lower in those that practice gratitude.

- **Lower Blood Pressure.** People that show and feel gratitude register with systolic blood pressures 10 percent lower and diastolic blood pressures 16 percent lower than those that don't feel grateful.

This is just the tip of the iceberg on the amazing effects gratitude can have on your physical person. Less fatigue, reduced chronic pain, better energy ... there is a wellspring of benefits to practicing gratitude on a daily basis.

Using Gratitude in Your Own Life

Gratitude is something everyone from every walk of life can practice. It doesn't cost anything and can greatly enrich lives. It can take a little practice to get into the habit of regularly showing gratitude, but with some help, you will be well on your way to a happier, kinder, more healthy existence.

Gratitude isn't a difficult habit to form, and it's a heck of a lot healthier than most! With practice you'll find that your whole way of thinking will shift. You'll notice the beauty in little things and be able to better handle the bigger things when they come along. I have laid out a workbook of seven gratitude exercises to get you started.

I encourage you to use these and build upon them. Once you get into the habit of feeling grateful, you'll find yourself spreading the infectious state of positivity!